Wesley
Gets a New Home

ISBN 979-8-88540-791-5 (paperback)
ISBN 979-8-88540-792-2 (digital)

Copyright © 2023 by Connie Erisman

All rights reserved. No part of this publication may be reproduced, distributed, or transmitted in any form or by any means, including photocopying, recording, or other electronic or mechanical methods without the prior written permission of the publisher. For permission requests, solicit the publisher via the address below.

Christian Faith Publishing
832 Park Avenue
Meadville, PA 16335
www.christianfaithpublishing.com

Printed in the United States of America

Wesley Gets a New Home

Connie Erisman

It was a beautiful spring morning in the Ozarks. The smell of new grass filled the air as the cattle grazed in the pasture. A brand-new baby calf was lying next to his mom. His mom was not well, and baby calf did not know what to do.

A few days later, the baby calf was wandering all alone in the field when a family drove up to the gate and looked lovingly at him. His momma had died, and the baby calf had no family. He was very sad.

Two children got out of the truck and carefully walked up to the baby calf. Their daddy, farmer Jake, whisked baby calf up into his arms and carried him to the truck. It was a long ride on farmer Jake's lap, but baby calf would soon understand why he had to leave the pasture.

4

This family seemed nice to baby calf. "I wonder where they are taking me. I am hungry," he said.

Soon, the truck motor stopped. The two children, Blaine and Taylen, were so excited to bring the baby calf to their home. They searched and searched their minds for a good name. Taylen finally decided that the baby calf's name should be Wesley!

The baby calf was excited to finally get a name. He was especially happy to get out of the truck and be carried to his new pen. Farmer Jake made it just for him. Fresh straw made a nice place for Wesley to lay.

Taylen and Blaine quickly, with the help of their mom and dad, stirred up a big bottle of warm milk for Wesley. Poor Wesley did not understand at first what was in the bottle. Momma Lacey placed her fingers in his mouth to suck, which helped Wesley learn to drink from a bottle. He quickly latched on as soon as he got a taste of the sweet milk.

His tail wagged happily as he gulped down the delicious meal his new family had prepared for him. When his tummy was full, he gazed at his new family.

They looked different from the cows back at his other home. They smelled different too.

Every day, Taylen or Blaine would leave their house to walk down to Wesley's pen to give him his breakfast before school and after school. Wesley was very thankful. He missed his mom, but he was starting to really like his new family.

They grew to love Wesley. They would put a halter and lead rope on him and take him for walks. Wesley enjoyed going for walks. He especially liked all of the hugs and rubs that his new family gave him.

Wesley grew stronger and happier. He was excited to see the children each day. Soon Wesley was jumping and running with Taylen and Blaine. He knew his name and would come whenever the children called out to him.

A few months passed, and Wesley was getting bigger. He needed more room to roam and play. He now ate grass when he went for walks with the children. And boy did he like the tasty sweet grain that his new family now gave him.

One day, Farmer Jake and Momma Lacey loaded Wesley up into the truck to go for a ride. It was time for him to get to live with the other cows in a big pasture again. Wesley was sad at first. He wanted to get back into the truck and return to his little pen. But farmer Jake knew this was best for Wesley.

Blaine and Taylen visited Wesley almost every day.

Wesley would run toward the gate when he heard the sound of the truck pulling in. The children called his name as Wesley would run right up to the truck. Blaine and Taylen would get out and play with Wesley. He would run around them happily and rub up next to them. Wesley loved his new family even if they looked different and smelled different too.

Farmer Jake's family had taken very good care of Wesley, and he was now part of their family. They visit him regularly at the pasture. Wesley comes running from the woods when he hears them calling his name. Wesley still gets a big bottle of fresh milk on occasion when his new family visits him.

Sometimes, we lose special ones in our lives, but like Wesley, we can love a new family too.

About the Author

Connie Erisman is a wife, mother, and grandmother who enjoys working with young people. She has served as a counselor and board member for a Bible camp for over thirty-five years and loves encouraging children. Connie experienced the loss of her father as a young teen and knows the pain of loss and the joys of having a wonderful stepfather, similar to her narrative about her character, Wesley. Giving hope to those who hurt is dear to her heart.

Connie has been a newspaper publisher for about thirty-eight years and works in marketing/sales for the business. She has written feature articles for the newspaper as well.

She loves people and sharing the love of God with others. Connie has been a speaker for various Christian women's events and has written articles for *Christian Woman magazine*.

Connie enjoys spending time with her grandchildren. She and her husband like hiking and spur of the moment adventures! She believes there is always beauty to see wherever you go. Connie attributes God to being a creative genius who gave us so much beauty if we just take the time to notice.

www.ingramcontent.com/pod-product-compliance
Lightning Source LLC
Chambersburg PA
CBHW041825110726
48006CB00019B/2515